The Spiritual Laws of ECK

MAHANTA

The Spiritual Laws of ECK

Harold Klemp

ECKANKAR
Minneapolis

Printed in U.S.A.
Library of Congress Catalog Card Number: 90-082505

Compiled by Myrtis Affeld

Edited by Joan Klemp
Anthony Moore
Mary Carroll Moore

Text illustrations by Signy Cohen

Third Printing—1997

Publisher's Cataloging-in-Publication
(Provided by Quality Books, Inc.)

Klemp, Harold.
The spiritual laws of ECK / Harold Klemp ; [with writings by Paul Twitchell ; compiled by Myrtis Affeld ; edited by Joan Klemp, Anthony Moore and Mary Carroll Moore ; text illustrations by Signy Cohen].—1st ed.
p. cm.
Includes bibliographical references.
Preassigned LCCN: 90-82505.
ISBN: 1-57043-046-2

1. Eckankar (Organization) 2. Spiritual life—Eckankar (Organization) I. Title.

BP605.E3K54 1997   299'.93
                         QBI97-40729

♾ The paper used in this publication meets the minimum requirements of the American National Standard for Information Sciences — Permanence of Paper for Printed Library Materials, ANSI Z39.48-1984.

The basic principle of Soul Travel is that man is the Spirit self, that he can take charge of the Soul body and can move from the visible planes into the invisible worlds at will. When he becomes proficient at this, the beneficial results are freedom, charity, and wisdom. These are the God-qualities lying latent in each Soul, which must be brought to Soul's attention in order to unfold the true self in all Its glory.

—Paul Twitchell,
ECKANKAR—The Key to Secret Worlds

Contents

Foreword ix

Laws of Wisdom—The laws that speak of divine
power and how it manifests in the universe.

    Causation 3
    Consciousness 5
    God.. 9
    Grace 13
    HU 15
    Life.. 17
    Mksha... 19
    Physical Universe 21
    Soul... 23
    Spirit... 25
    Spiritual Nonperfection 27
    Three Basic Principles of Eckankar 29

Laws of Freedom—The practical laws that afford
a smoother passage through everyday life.

    Attitudes 33
    Balance 39
    Detachment... 43
    Economy 47
    Facsimiles 53

Invisible Laws 55
Karma 57
Nature 63
Polarity 65
Reversed Effort 71
Unity 73
Vibration 75

Laws of Charity—The laws that bring Soul a greater capacity to love.

Chela, Laws and Rules for the 81
Creativity 83
Danda, the Righteous Law 87
Dharma 91
Four Zoas 95
Love 97
Noninterference 101
Silence 103

Glossary 105
Bibliography 107

Foreword

The teachings of ECK define the nature of Soul. You are Soul, a particle of God sent into the worlds (including earth) to gain spiritual experience.

The goal in ECK is spiritual freedom in this lifetime, after which you become a Co-worker with God, both here and in the next world. Karma and reincarnation are primary beliefs.

Key to the ECK teachings is the Mahanta, the Living ECK Master. He has the special ability to act as both the Inner and Outer Master for ECK students. He is the prophet of Eckankar, given respect but not worship. He teaches the sacred name of God, HU, which lifts you spiritually into the Light and Sound of God, the ECK (Holy Spirit). Purified by the practice of the Spiritual Exercises of ECK, you are then able to accept the full love of God in this lifetime.

Sri Harold Klemp is the Mahanta, the Living ECK Master. He has written many books, discourses, and articles about the spiritual life. Many of his public talks are available on audio- and videocassette. His teachings uplift people and help them recognize and understand their own experiences in the Light and Sound of God.

This book contains thought-provoking quotations from Sri Harold Klemp and from Paul Twitchell, the modern-day founder of Eckankar. Within these pages are many excellent tools to enliven your personal spiritual study and path to mastership.

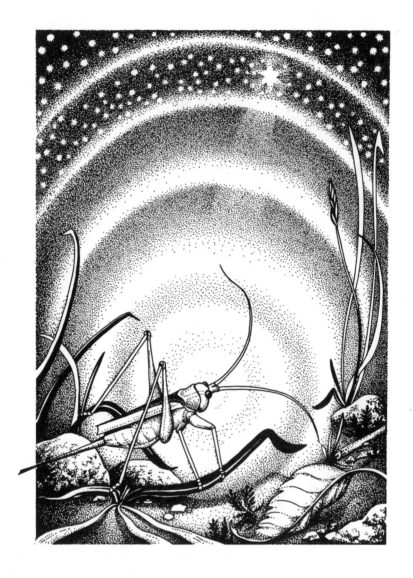

All things from heaven to earth are under Its care; and It hears the faint chirp of the cricket, though It may seem deaf to our loudest prayers.

Laws of Wisdom

The laws that speak of divine power and how
it manifests in the universe.

Causation

causation. The wheel of life, which is a factor in the human and spiritual cycles of lives; karma.

ECKANKAR Dictionary, p. 21

The ECK Power is the intelligence which pervades all space and animates all living things; this mental action and reaction is the Law of Causation. The principle of causation does not begin in the individual but in the cosmic power. It is not an objective faculty but a subjective process, and the results are seen in an infinite variety of conditions and experiences.

In order to express life there must be the power. Nothing can exist without the cosmic power. Everything which exists is some manifestation of this basic power from which and by which all things have been created and continually are being recreated.

Man lives in a fathomless sea of this plastic ether called the ECK Power; and this substance is ever alive and active. It is sensitive to the highest degree. Thought form takes mould or matrix from that which the substance expresses.

Dialogues with the Master, pp. 127–28

The other aspect of Spirit, even more important than the Light, is that which we know as the Sound. This Sound Current is actually the Voice of God, spoken of in the Bible as the Word: "In the beginning was the

Word. . . . And the word was made flesh, and dwelt among us." This Voice, the creative current which comes from God, has created the lower worlds. It comes out like a radio wave from a central broadcasting station. It's like a pebble thrown into a quiet lake, causing ripples to go out. These waves go out but they must always come back to the center; it's the returning wave that we are interested in. This is what Soul is looking for: to return to the God center. When It returns to the God center, we call this God-Realization, or the God Consciousness.

How to Find God, **Mahanta Transcripts, Book 2, p. 156**

Someone wrote to me from a farm in Africa. He said a hen laiḍ a bunch of eggs that were fertilized by a funny-looking rooster whose head and neck were bald. Every time the rooster would come in the yard, the family would all laugh at it.

It was all pretty funny until the eggs hatched. One of the chicks came out looking exactly like the rooster—bald head, bald neck. Because the little thing was so ugly and small, the other chicks picked on it and finally even broke its leg. To protect it, the family had to bring it into the house.

The person who wrote the letter said, "You know, it's interesting how we laughed at this rooster that was bald-headed and bald-necked, and now all of a sudden we find that one just like him has taken up residence in our home!"

Thoughts of any nature are going to come home to roost. This is called the Law of Karma, or the Law of Cause and Effect. The ECKists are quite familiar with it.

How to Find God, **Mahanta Transcripts, pp. 303–4**

Consciousness

Consciousness, Law of. The recognition, or realization, of the beingness of self or thing in thought, which manifests external life and form.

ECKANKAR Dictionary, p. 25

Everything in the universe has its origin in idea, in thought, and it has its completion in the manifestation of thought through form. Many intermediate stages are necessary, but the cause and effect of the series are the thought and the thing. This shows that in essence the thing already existed in thought. . . . This is consciousness. If it is a true fact that the thing must be in thought before thought can form the thing, then it is plain that the Divine ideal can only be externalized in our objective life to the proportion it is first formed in our thought. It takes form from our thought only to the extent we have apprehended its existence in the Divine ECK. . . .

Soul is the thinker of thoughts. The consciousness responds when directed by Soul, which is beyond all thought, beyond all matter, energy, space and time. The very act of thinking imposes self-consciousness because all thoughts are possible only through self-consciousness. Therefore, that which I am, that which is above and beyond all thoughts, cannot be revealed by the consciousness nor the intellect. Even when the consciousness cannot think of it, it is possible for Soul,

5

which I am, to know the whole thing in a complete way. . . .

In the creative process of Soul we become the individual reflection of what we realize the Divine Power to be, relative to one's self. If we realize the Divine as the infinite potential of all that can constitute a perfect human being, this conception must, by the Law of Creativity, gradually build up a corresponding image in our thoughts, which in turn, will act on our external condition.

This, by the law of consciousness, is the nature of the process.

The Flute of God, pp. 124–25

We each choose our own state of consciousness. It takes a while for many individuals, even many ECK initiates, to recognize this. We make our own worlds. What we are today is the sum total of everything we have thought or been throughout the ages.

How to Find God, Mahanta Transcripts, Book 2, p. 8

All paths to God are provided by Spirit for the express purpose of giving Soul in Its varying states of consciousness a choice in how It wants to return to God. Each path leads to another path, and then to another. It is one thing to be born into a certain state of consciousness, but we owe it to ourselves to make the effort to reach higher and beyond. Upon birth, we are given whatever consciousness we need to get from birth to death; the kind that allows us to go to school, learn a trade or a profession, and make our way. But it takes a special effort to go beyond and reach greater states of consciousness. We can do this by direct experience with the Light and Sound of Spirit.

How to Find God, Mahanta Transcripts, Book 2, p. 121

Every time you move into another state of consciousness, your nutritional laws may change. Then you start juggling your diet and vitamins. When you finally lose track, you may end up going to a nutritionist. Why? Because you are going through different states of consciousness and your body is responding to the law, As above, so below. As you grow in your state of consciousness or as you come nearer to another initiation, things begin to change and you wonder what's happening. It's simply that your state of consciousness is changing. Even your word, your secret word, may not work anymore, and you must ask to find a new one.

How to Find God, **Mahanta Transcripts, Book 2, p. 226**

God

God, Law of. Everything has its origin in Spirit; divine truth is one and unchanging.

ECKANKAR Dictionary, **p. 57**

The odyssey of Soul teaches us to cooperate with the laws of God. It takes many lifetimes of bumps and bruises before all the lessons of Godhood sink in. And when they do, we are granted the grace to partake consciously of the highest aspects of sainthood.

The Living Word, **p. 199**

The Law of God states that "Soul has existence because God wills it." Thus, God loves all life so dearly that It allows Soul to exist. If It did not love life, there would be no life-forms in this universe and all would be barren. Time, space, law, chance, matter, primitive energy, and intelligence are only the effects of God's love for life, and only exist to serve Soul in Its journey to find liberation and freedom.

The Soul is not the cause for the law which brings happiness or misery. Not being free, neither does It act as the prime cause that brings about the opposite. As the free Self It has the opportunity to establish Itself as the prime mover for bringing about happiness and letting life be what it should be. It does not establish life but exists because life itself supports Soul

9

as the prime consideration of God's love for every individual Soul within the universe.

The Shariyat-Ki-Sugmad, **Book One, p. 153**

There was a time before these lower worlds were created when Soul resided in the heavens. It's difficult to conceive of such a thing in heaven as a selfish, or ungrowing, Soul; but interestingly enough, It wouldn't serve anyone or anything except Itself. And so God sent Soul down into the lower worlds which had been created specifically for Its experience. The hardships and troubles, even the happiness and joy—the full spectrum of experience that we know through the five senses and beyond—are for Soul's unfoldment, so that one day It may become a Co-worker with God. This is the only purpose of it all.

How to Find God, **Mahanta Transcripts, Book 2, p. 223**

Spiritual enlightenment and illumination come as we have contact with this Light and Sound of God. The ECKist sees the actual Light of God that comes during contemplation. It gives spiritual upliftment and takes away the karma which has been created throughout our past lives and the daily karma from this lifetime.

We can do without the Light but we can't do without the Sound. It is an actual sound that we hear. It may be that of an orchestra; it may be that of a flute. . . .

This is the only way that God can speak to us, through either the Light or the Sound. Whenever we have an experience on the inner and we hear a booming voice, it may be a Master, whether seen or unseen, another being, or an angel of God—but it's not God. The true Voice is what we seek. It gives the wisdom and the truth which surpasses all understanding.

10

As we begin to get this Light and Sound in our life, it shows in how we conduct our daily affairs. Our daily life is a reflection of what happens inwardly. We may be spiritually successful, but it doesn't necessarily mean we're going to be rich. If we set a goal for a project, we ought to get a grasp of spiritual principles from the experience. These help us succeed in the sense that these experiences take us to the next step in life. What we call success, other people may call failure, because we have a different viewpoint. And because we have this viewpoint, we have happiness and lightness which many other people would dearly love to experience but have never found.

How to Find God, **Mahanta Transcripts, Book 2, p. 241**

God, of Itself, runs a straight course and does not take care of the individual, in a sense, yet It has the individual's welfare close to Its heart. All things from heaven to earth are under Its care; and It hears the faint chirp of the cricket, though It may seem deaf to our loudest prayers.

So we are appointed as ECK Gurus to take care of all who come for help. "Lo, you who are weary and burdened come unto me and I will take your burden." Remember that? This is our responsibility in life.

The Living ECK Master, the Godman who is now living in this physical universe, cares for all life. Trust in him.

The Key to ECKANKAR, **p. 15**

One of the most prevalent misunderstandings is that the Law of God works only for those who have a devout or religious objective. This is a fallacy. It works just as impersonally as any law of physics. It

11

can be used for greed or selfish purposes, as well as noble ones.

The Key to ECKANKAR, p. 16

The greatest principle of God is the survival of the individual, that is, Soul. The dynamic principle of existence is survival.

The Key to ECKANKAR, p. 27

Let it be known, here and now, that all knowledge and all wisdom are never given to Soul. For the world of God is without beginning and without ending, infinite in all attributes and qualities, and constantly expanding towards greater truth and greater wisdom.

The Key to ECKANKAR, p. 29

12

Grace

Grace, Law of. To be in accord with the ways of the Sugmad for making each a divine channel, through working in the area of nonattachment mainly through discipline of the emotions.

ECKANKAR Dictionary, **p. 58**

We take our steps on the spiritual path; we climb the ladder to God. Jesus said, "Come unto me and be lifted up." What he tried to explain was simply this: The grace of God does not descend upon us. This is something that religions often do not understand. They feel the grace of God comes to us merely because we ask. It does in a way, but first we must earn it. We must make at least some effort before the grace of God comes to us; but when it does, we are lifted up into it.

How to Find God, **Mahanta Transcripts, Book 2, p. 8**

You have to undergo the discipline to lift your state of consciousness to an area where these teachers are, where they can help you. In a sense, we are led to believe that the grace of God descends upon us, but actually it's as Jesus spoke of when he told his followers to come unto him and he would lift them up.

How to Find God, **Mahanta Transcripts, Book 2, p. 48**

Grace

Anyone with a sufficient desire for a realization of God can achieve that realization—the grace of God will guarantee it.

The Key to ECKANKAR, p. 41

HU

HU, Law of. Spirit is the all-penetrating power which is the forming power of the universes of HU, the Voice of HU.

ECKANKAR Dictionary, p. 65

The path of ECK is to lead an individual into a life that is spiritually uplifting and never degrading or depraved in any manner. It's supposed to build. When you get something on the inner—a direction to do something—if it's positive and harmonious, then do it. If you feel upset by it or if it demands that you exercise power over another person—in other words, the command you get means someone else loses his freedom to act as he wants to—then don't do it. It's the negative power, and it can even take the face of the ECK Master. Why? For our experience, so that we learn how to challenge it with one of the sacred words of God, such as HU. You can chant this quietly, and you can have protection. It opens you for this protection from Spirit.

This is one of the functions of HU, and it's a very useful tool. You can do it at any time. If you need help—maybe somebody's gossiping or attacking you— you don't direct it at them but you just chant to uplift yourself spiritually so that you either gain an understanding or to protect yourself or whatever's needed.

How to Find God, **Mahanta Transcripts, Book 2, p. 78**

15

Many of the different religious teachings have initiations. The Masonic order speaks of the lost word. This lost word actually is the sound of HU, or the Sound of God. This is one of the sacred names of God, which is a charged word. Such a word—and this includes our personal word—does not have power in itself. The word which we are given during the initiation acts like a key to unlock the protection and the spiritual help that is available from the ECK, or the Mahanta. We chant or sing this word, quietly or out loud, whenever we have need of this help.

***How to Find God,* Mahanta Transcripts, Book 2, pp. 89–90**

HU, the secret name of God . . . can be chanted or sung quietly to yourself when you are in trouble or when you need consolation in time of grief. It gives strength, it gives health, it opens you as a channel for the greater healing of Divine Spirit.

***How to Find God,* Mahanta Transcripts, Book 2, p. 313**

The Sound of God, the Audible Life Stream, is the purifying element which uplifts Soul, so that one day It may return home to God, Its creator.

***How to Find God,* Mahanta Transcripts, Book 2, p. 314**

Life

life. Being; the experience of states of consciousness; life is Spirit, and Spirit is static; the Sound; the ECK.

ECKANKAR Dictionary, p. 88

Each new experience, each new situation of life, widens the outlook of the chela and brings about a subtle transformation within himself. Thus the nature of every chela who is earnest and serious about the works of ECK is changing constantly, not only on account of the conditions of life, but by the constant addition of new impressions, the structure of the mind becomes ever more diverse and complex. Whether it is called progress or degeneration, depends upon how one looks at it. But it has to be admitted that this is the law of life, in which the spiritual and the psychic coordinate and balance one another in the world of the spirito-materialistic, where Soul must serve out Its time for perfection.

The Shariyat-Ki-Sugmad, Book Two, p. 104

Why me, Lord? is the age-old question we ask God. It is a form of prayer; it covers up our ignorance of the laws of life. Problems with life occur when we don't understand the laws of ECK—the laws of Spirit.

The Golden Heart, Mahanta Transcripts, Book 4, p. 2

Every issue of life is determined not by external conditions and things, but by one's consciousness. For example, the body in and of itself has no power, no intelligence, and is not responsible for its actions. A hand left to itself would remain where it is forever. There must be something to move it, and that something we call "I" or "Spirit." That "I" determines how the hand will be used; the hand cannot determine that in and of itself. The hand exists as an effect or as a form and responds to direction. As a vehicle or tool, it is obedient to us, and we impart to it whatever usefulness it has.

This idea can be applied to other parts of the body. The consciousness that formed the body in the beginning is the consciousness that maintains and sustains it. God gave us dominion through consciousness, and this consciousness, which is the creative principle of our body, must also be its sustaining and maintaining principle.

Once you have this principle, you have caught the entire principle of life. Literally, this is the Law of Life: the substance, the activity, the intelligent direction of life which is within man.

The Key to ECKANKAR, pp. 18–19

It is the law of all life to either progress or degenerate.

The Shariyat-Ki-Sugmad, Book Two, p. 198

Mksha

Mksha, Law of. *MUHK-shah* Life is only Spirit, and being Spirit it has nothing; it has only intelligence with the peculiar ability to perceive, penetrate, and survive, and have causation, specialization, creativeness, beauty, love, and ethics.

ECKANKAR Dictionary, p. 99

There are fundamental laws that govern this physical universe through Spirit. These were once taught by an ancient ECK sage named Mksha, who appeared on this earth some 35,000 years ago to teach the people of the Indus Valley. His first teaching was, "Life is only Spirit, and being spirit it has nothing." The understanding of this points out clearly that it has only intelligence with the peculiar ability to perceive, penetrate, survive, have causation, specialization, creativeness, beauty, love and ethics.

Spirit is the all-penetrating power which is the forming power of the universes of HU. It is the immortal unchanging source of life which only changes form regardless of what the world may be. It is the causative force which man has studied, written about, and can only know the exacting properties of, never actually acquiring total knowledge. We know that its modus operandi works peculiarly in exacting ways as do the mathematical formulas. Scientists and students of the Holy Works, all know this.

The Flute of God, p. 86

Physical Universe

laws of the physical universe. The Book of Laws; seven fundamental laws that govern the physical universe through Spirit: Law of Attitudes, Law of Facsimiles, Law of HU, Law of Polarity, Law of Soul, Law of Unity, and Law of Vibrations.

ECKANKAR Dictionary, **p. 87**

One must come to realize that all creation is finished in the lower universes. Creativeness is only a deeper receptiveness. The entire contents of all time and all space, while experienced in a time sequence, actually coexist in an infinite and eternal *now.* In fact, all that mankind ever was or ever shall be in these lower worlds exists *now!* This is what is meant by the statement that creation is finished. Nothing is ever created, only manifested. What is called creativeness is only becoming aware of what already *is.* You simply become increasingly aware of portions of that which already exists.

The Key to ECKANKAR, **p. 7**

Soul

Soul, Law of. Soul is the manifested individual beingness of the ECK Spirit. It has free will, opinions, intelligence, imagination, and immortality.

ECKANKAR Dictionary, p. 138

Soul is the manifested individual beingness of this ECK Spirit. The individual Soul has been created out of this Spirit, with the ability to have free will, to make its own choice, to be able to have opinions, intelligence, imagination, and to postulate and create.

The Flute of God, p. 87

This means that all Souls who enter into the heavenly state must abide by the law which they establish for themselves. The self-abiding law is for the individual Soul to recognize that It is Its own law. First of all, It must love or give out goodwill to all beings within the heavenly worlds. Secondly, It must make Its own law to abide by, and this must be in harmony with the great law: Love all things.

The Shariyat-Ki-Sugmad, Book Two, p. 138

We recognize that Soul is eternal; It has no beginning and no ending. Therefore, when a person leaves this physical body, he continues to exist, usually on a higher plane of consciousness.

How to Find God, Mahanta Transcripts, Book 2, p. 48

Spirit

Spirit, Law of. Spirit, in Itself, is the principle of increase; future conditions grow out of present conditions; there is always something more to come, another experience to experience.

ECKANKAR Dictionary, **p. 139**

Self-mastery simply means that a person has the ability to run his own life according to the laws of Spirit. This presumes, first of all, that you know the laws of Spirit. The understanding of these laws comes through the Light and Sound of God; it is a direct infusion of the Shariyat-Ki-Sugmad into Soul.

The Golden Heart, **Mahanta Transcripts, Book 4, p. 74**

Spirit is the all-penetrating power which is the forming power of the universes of HU. It is the immortal unchanging source of life which only changes form regardless of what the world may be. . . .

This Spirit, the Voice of HU—HU is often known as the Sugmad—which is the true name of God in the upper realms, has one great quality and that is to create effect. As It flows down through the worlds, from Its fountainhead in the center of all creation, far above this earth world, It needs distributors, and It works through Souls.

The Flute of God, **p. 86**

Our name for Spirit is simply ECK. This ECK is what the Bible refers to as the Holy Ghost, the Comforter. This is the same manifestation that came to the apostles at Pentecost. They heard a sound like a rushing wind. This is one of the sounds of Spirit. There are many more, such as the sound of the flute.

How to Find God, **Mahanta Transcripts, Book 2, p. 40**

The Sound and Light are the twin aspects of Spirit. This is the Voice of God. There are three parts, actually, that we are interested in as we step on the spiritual path. First there is thought. We use our mind and the imaginative techniques in working with the Spiritual Exercises of ECK. With the Spiritual Exercises of ECK, we consciously try to make contact with this Light and Sound of God. It's a worthwhile goal to experience the Voice of God: It means we have contact with the Divinity.

How to Find God, **Mahanta Transcripts, Book 2, p. 72**

This only means that God of Itself is Being, and Spirit is that extension of It into all universes, and you, as the instrument, are Spirit made flesh.

The Key to ECKANKAR, **p. 8**

In ECK, the individual is instructed in the laws of Spirit. How he uses this knowledge determines how soon he enters the joyful state of God Enlightenment, which can be attained while still in the human body.

The Living Word, **p. 36**

Spiritual Nonperfection

"The Law of Spiritual Nonperfection holds that no one ever becomes a perfect being." There is always one more step in God's plan of conscious evolution. This is all the more true of spiritual things which always seek, but never find, completion.

Child in the Wilderness, p. 250

This creative process depends upon the spiritual unfoldment of Soul and the degree of Its awakened consciousness. . . . This is also in accord with the Law of Spiritual Evolution, which presupposes inequality in all things and beings and their continued effort for self-improvement in life.

The Spiritual Notebook, p. 57

Three Basic Principles of Eckankar

By now he begins to see the wisdom of the three basic principles of ECK. First, Soul is eternal. It has no beginning nor ending. Second, whosoever travels the high path of ECK always dwells in the spiritual planes. Third, Soul always lives in the present. It has no past and no future, but always lives in the present moment.

The Shariyat-Ki-Sugmad, Book Two, p. 243

Out of these principles springs the doctrine and philosophy of ECK. There is nothing more to say and there is nothing less to say.

By the realization of these three principles the chela becomes a transparency for the divine impulse. He comes into a greater awareness of the divine plan in this world, and his part in it. He now rests in the arms of the Mahanta, the Inner ECK Master, and relies upon him to give him his divine guidance.

As he rises higher in this spiritual realization, the great discovery of life is found. The majestic law of God upon which the three principles of ECK rest is that "Soul exists because the Sugmad wills it."

The Shariyat-Ki Sugmad, Book One, pp. 155–56

We see the height of the mountains and the depths of the valleys, because the only way anything can be known in these lower worlds is in comparison to its oppposite.

Laws of Freedom

The practical laws that afford a smoother
passage through everyday life.

Attitudes

Attitudes, Law of. The fifth law of the physical universe, or Law of the States of Being; the power of imagination rules over will in the actions in this universe.

ECKANKAR Dictionary, p. 13

The fifth law of the physical universe is the Law of Attitudes, or the states of being. Frankly, everything that operates with the laws of this part is capable of performing miracles. Not will, but the power of imagination rules our actions in this universe.

The Flute of God, pp. 93–94

Lai Tsi says, "I have learned to stand back and let the divine work through me." We find that this is the simple way of doing it. . . .

I found when adopting a certain attitude that I made contact with this power. It was an attitude of curious, childlike devotion to the great Spirit. . . . So many people want this childlike state but the urgency of their physical needs causes tension and fear thus closing the channel between themselves and the Spirit. Anxiety and fear are tense emotions, fastening the person rigidly into the emotional plane of consciousness so that he cannot reach the spiritual plane where things come true.

Competition intensifies the attitude of tension; tension springs from fear; fear rises out of excessive self-love; excessive self-love cuts one off from the contact with the ECK; thus, the qualities leading to satisfaction, happiness and growth are not achieved. . . . Anyone who recognizes his own self, as Soul, relaxes at once, for he can truly say, "I and the Father are one." In this relaxed way, all channels from within are opened.

The Flute of God, pp. 94–95

Briefly, the Law of Attitudes goes like this. It is the corrected feeling and pictures you carry in your mind constantly. If you decide to take a picture with a camera—let's say of a tree, and do so, you view the pictured tree in the viewfinder. After a few days you get the pictures back from the camera shop, and you are not surprised to find that it's really a picture of a tree you took.

This is, simply, the same way life works. When we think, when we image something in our minds, we are sighting pictures in the viewfinder of the mind. The thought vibrations within us will deal with the exposed films we have made and presently the finished picture comes into visibility in our lives. It's as simple as that.

The Flute of God, p. 95

Every present thought solidifies into a future condition.

Dialogues with the Master, p. 50

Remember that the subtle forces within man are the same, but the important thing is the manner in which we call upon it. If we speak to it in negative terms, it responds in that manner. We impose self-limitations upon ourselves to give the power an opportunity to work through the subconscious mind.

Dialogues with the Master, **p. 60**

This is the attitude we take in life on the path to God. We don't say, "I'm afraid to step out in life because I'll be shown up as ignorant." We step out boldly and courageously. We learn things. We're willing to make a fool of ourself just for the sake of experience or learning.

How to Find God, **Mahanta Transcripts, Book 2, p. 18**

In ECK we understand that the mind runs in a rut. We pick up habits as children, which carry into the teen years and become hardened and solidified as we grow older. Anger and other attitudes of the mind stem from these habits. The only thing that is greater than mind is Soul. It is above the power of the mind, and It is the only thing able to nudge the mind out of its rut.

How to Find God, **Mahanta Transcripts, Book 2, p. 25**

We know that we can shape our future.... because the future is unformed. You can make it what you want, but first you have to be able to visualize what you want very clearly. Unfortunately, most people look for materialistic goals such as money, health, wealth, and companionship. But again I'm going to mention this: As Jesus said, "Seek ye first the Kingdom of God ... and all these things shall be added unto you." Make sure that your goal is worth the trouble.

To develop this creative imagination, work with the Spiritual Exercises of ECK. Experiment freely with these techniques. What you're looking for is to have experience with the Sound and Light, where you will have adventures in the other worlds.

How to Find God, **Mahanta Transcripts, Book 2, p. 51**

The mind with its routines and habits doesn't want to change what it has been doing. It wants to keep reading and enjoying itself. But Spirit moves on, and the mind and emotions and everything else move along. If we aren't willing to exercise this randomity . . . , we have a hard time through our initiations.

Going from one initiation level to the next ought to be a very easy and smooth transition. We have to be willing to let go of old attitudes and stay very open to Spirit as It tries to lead us into greater awareness. Once you have opened up to Spirit, the Inner Master will step in—as long as you give permission—and take you into the greater vistas. If Soul has given permission but the lower bodies don't know it, this is when you start saying you've got all these problems.

Now is the time to start giving of yourself. It doesn't necessarily have to be within the ECK program, but you have to begin giving back to life in some way. Do this according to your own talents and interests. Some people like to give talks, others don't; they're petrified. If that's the case, then don't give talks. Some like to work with children, while others—maybe those who have been parents—may say, I've done my time; let someone else have a turn.

How to Find God, **Mahanta Transcripts, Book 2, p. 69**

It is I AM's concept of Itself that determines the form and scenery of Its existence. Everything depends upon Its attitude towards Itself; that which It will not affirm as true of Itself cannot awaken in Its world.

The Key to ECKANKAR, **p. 6**

A mind with randomity . . . can change under any circumstance—this is a factor which isn't very well known. But the higher Soul travels on the spiritual path, the less become Its burdens, and the easier it is to change swiftly from one course to another. A mind that moves with random speed works in the field of randomity.

The Key to ECKANKAR, **p. 9**

We do not have to please God, we have to manifest Its presence.

Many who are doing good have little or no idea as to what good really is. Many are willing to have God interfere in their lives, but are not willing to do what is needed for themselves. However, when anyone examines his life, he will come to the realization that it is always his beliefs, considerations, and conditionings that determine his experiences in life.

So we come to the most important part of life's message: It is not what we do that determines our experience in life, but it is what we expect! Even when you have done all the correct things, if you have the haunting fear that things will go wrong, they will go wrong. Is it because you are bad, sinful, or evil? No. It is because you have that belief.

The Key to ECKANKAR, **p. 14**

Whatever is in the consciousness is bound to come forth. . . .

It can be compulsive or of the free will. The covert negative attitudes that one has against another or against certain segments of life will leap out in time. For example, if a person has many covert attitudes against men and women, it is doubtful if he can confront his fellowmen. This is the type of person who spends too much time alone.

Don't do too many things with people of this nature, like precipitating their anger, because it will definitely pull their triggers and they will go down the dwindling spiral in a hurry. Some cases are suicides. The karma created out of some action against someone else keeps the individuals in a constant quarrel, mainly with themselves. Many times they believe they are quarreling with another, but it is with themselves.

The Key to ECKANKAR, p. 19

Balance

Balance, Law of. The stability which lies in the Godhead: all is completely in balance in God's universal body. The principle of unity, of oneness, but in the lower worlds this unity is simulated by the interchange between the pairs of opposites.

ECKANKAR Dictionary, **p. 15**

This blindness to cause-and-effect is still man's relentless problem today. The human consciousness refuses to admit that all actions have consequences. The Living ECK Master demonstrates the Law of Balance in terms of contemporary customs.

The Living Word, **p. 164**

As we live the life of ECK, we want to know how It works in our daily life. A professional musician recently said he had developed a case of jittery nerves. So much of this creative flow was coming through him that he was not able to take the time to balance it with some kind of physical activity. . . . He's so involved with his music that he has not been able to work any physical activity into his daily schedule.

Another musician told about joining a basketball team. The musician was able to get his exercise in this way. It is important to keep a balance in our physical life. When we get the ECK flowing in, all too often we want to put all of our attention on the books of ECK or the contemplative exercises, and we forget that we also have to live day to day.

How to Find God, **Mahanta Transcripts, Book 2, p. 27**

Life goes up and down. We have times when everything is going our way, but there are also times when we're at the bottom. If we keep ourselves open to Spirit, there will be an equal balance. This is what is meant by the detached state: When our fortunes hit bottom, we surrender to Spirit. Then we can go back up more naturally, and we'll maintain this rhythm of life. As life goes on around us, the detached state is that which runs right through the center; we are the balanced individual working in the Soul consciousness.

How to Find God, **Mahanta Transcripts, Book 2, p. 31**

We do what we can, but we don't feel guilty and we don't let ourselves get out of balance. We work with other like-minded people to accomplish things; we don't sit back in life and just wash our hands of the whole affair.

How to Find God, **Mahanta Transcripts, Book 2, p. 53**

You get to the Soul Plane by balancing the positive and the negative parts within yourself; they come into perfect balance on the Soul Plane. From this moment on we have Self-Realization. . . . This is a spiritual transfiguration that occurs—you actually become a new person. You are now in the state of self-recognition: knowing who you are, what you are, and what your mission in life may be.

How to Find God, **Mahanta Transcripts, Book 2, p. 63**

Each Soul is an individual and unique being. In the lower planes we have the two parts of our lower nature: the positive and the negative. When we get to the Soul Plane, we find that these two parts become one. This is called the self-recognition state, what Socrates referred to when he said, "Man, know thyself." Up until this time, knowing the self meant merely knowing the ego, or the little self, rather than our true spiritual nature. Our consciousness changes when we reach the Soul Plane; we now have an outlook on life that is balanced.

In the dream state, marriage simply means that Soul is having an inner initiation where the two parts of Itself are drawn a little closer together. We are looking for the linkup of Soul with the ECK, this Divine Spirit which comes from God. Each time you see a marriage on the inner planes, regardless of the personality you perceive as your mate, it means a closer marriage with Spirit and with God.

How to Find God, **Mahanta Transcripts, Book 2, pp. 185–86**

We don't want to practice austerities; that is not balance. Buddha spoke about this. He had started out his life as a rich young man, protected from seeing poverty or sorrow; and when he went out into the world, he said, Now I must beg and become poor. He tried fasting, and that didn't work out so well. All he got was skinny as a rail. After a while he said there must be some way to live a life that is well balanced. There must be a middle way.

In the spiritual life, we look to find the balance so that when we have this experience of God and see the Light—whether It is the Blue Light or anything else— we are able to carry on. We don't get frantic and say, Will I ever see It again? When the time is right, you will. Others will hear the Sound. These are the two aspects of God which the ECKists, and even those who aren't in Eckankar outwardly, are beginning to learn about and experience in their daily life.

How to Find God, Mahanta Transcripts, Book 2, p. 224

Someone mentioned they didn't know how to find people with motivation or how to motivate them. And really you can't. You find people who are motivated at any particular moment. Some are motivated for awhile, and then they go into a rest period — the rest points in eternity. There is a natural cycle that we run: activity, rest, activity, rest. An ECKist learns how to walk the middle path where he can make the activity and rest work for him, so that he becomes a conscious Co-worker with God twenty-four hours a day.

How to Find God, Mahanta Transcripts, Book 2, p. 337

Detachment

detachment. Giving up strong affection for the environment and possessions, but not ceasing to identify with them; becoming independent of them; mentally free from love of the world and all worldly desires.

ECKANKAR Dictionary, p. 33

The word detachment is too cold. What is meant in spiritual terms is this—we, as one with all, will have a certain amount of pleasure and pain, but will not let it affect our emotional balance too greatly to throw our minds into the extreme poles of joy or sorrow. The real control is detachment from fear. Once you have gained this important attribute of God, then you can enjoy greater life. Yes, you can have a joy mixed with pain and not be affected to the same extent as previously. Only when fear is in control of those two poles is your life attached to its physical, mental, and spiritual possessions. Give up fear and you need never give up another thing in your life. Great joys physically, mentally, and spiritually can become yours, balanced by what sorrows there need be in your life!

Dialogues with the Master, p. 79

The razor's edge is one's calm detachment from the things of this world; yet he may enjoy them as a blessing of life, for past karma has brought them for his experience. There is no virtue in suffering,

43

poverty, or martyrdom, unless the individual needs those experiences for the purification of Soul.

The Living Word, **p. 205**

No man can reach God practicing any path except devotion to the Sugmad through the Mahanta. One must be detached from all love of material things and events, from all concern about them. The chela attains this attitude—because his love is centered above the perishable things of this world—and reaches the heavenly planes.

From the love of objects of the senses man has desires; from his desires rises anger. From anger proceeds delusion, and from delusion come confused memories and senses. This destroys his love of God, and from all this he perishes. But when he is disciplined and places his love in the Mahanta, then does he move among the objects of his senses free from pleasures and free from pain, but mostly free from self-indulgence.

The Shariyat-Ki-Sugmad, **Book One, p. 136**

The vairag is the detached state of consciousness. This goes along with God-Realization. Detached does not mean without compassion, uncaring, without love. It means simply that you can have compassion, you can enjoy life, but if sorrow comes into your life, it does not burden you until the end of your days. You are able to see the hand of God in it.

How to Find God, **Mahanta Transcripts, Book 2, p. 22**

Charity is what the Christian Bible speaks of as good will. We call it vairag, or detachment.

How to Find God, **Mahanta Transcripts, Book 2, p. 40**

Detached means seeing the play of life—crying when we must, laughing when we can—but at all times looking at life from the viewpoint of Soul, knowing that even this shall pass away.

How to Find God, **Mahanta Transcripts, Book 2, p. 280**

Detached does not mean unemotional; it means that no matter what we have in life, we will not be crushed if it is taken from us. It means we have the attitude of total trust in life to give us what is for our own spiritual benefit.

How to Find God, **Mahanta Transcripts, Book 2, p. 351**

There are a few individuals who do drink from this water of immortality; they learn to work with the enzymes and to reverse the aging process because they have a mission. They are not concerned about staying in the body or not. They just do their work. The person who qualifies is one who learns to work in the state of vairag, or detachment. This does not mean giving up all interest in the family, throwing away all emotions and walking through life like a zombie, a computer-controlled robot, and then saying, I am now in the detached state. No. One who does that is actually in the sleep state.

Journey of Soul, **Mahanta Transcripts, Book 1, p. 198**

Economy

Service means that every move, every thought, everything we do gets the best advantage. No matter what thought we have or what action we take, it results in the most productive deed that we can do as Soul learning to become a Co-worker with God. I have often referred to this service as the Law of Economy. It means that in every way we look for the best. We look to excel in every way. If we are going to paint a picture, it will be the best we can do today. Yet tomorrow we will be able to do it better. If we write a book today, it's going to be great; but the book we write tomorrow will be even better. We use the Law of Economy: Only as many words as we need, and that's all.

How to Find God, **Mahanta Transcripts, Book 2, p. 351**

The Wayshower teaches . . . survival to his students in spiritual things. His simple methods are usually overlooked as he arranges the chela's karmic debts into some semblance of order. Karma due for repayment is fed back to his charges in accord with the Law of Economy.

The Living Word, **p. 81**

Many times we determine the value of something by the way it is presented and by its packaging. If it appears more attractive, we don't mind paying more for it. In doing so, however, we are not using our resources to the fullest, which is the Law of Economy.

The Book of ECK Parables, Volume 2, p. 154

Some messages just make good sense. "When you go out to buy, don't show your silver." That's the Law of Economy. A good spiritual reminder is this one, which demonstrates the returns of love: "If you continually give, you will continually have."

The Living Word, p. 177

There is something that I have been watching and studying for years, and it's one of the laws that is rarely mentioned. It's called the Law of Economy. The principle is referred to in some of the ECK books, but without that title. It merely means that you get the most mileage out of every gallon of gas. I get better mileage than I did before, but I still think it isn't running as fast as it could or as far as it could, because there is always another step.

The Secret Teachings, Mahanta Transcripts, Book 3, p. 46

The Law of Economy presupposes that everything we do is in harmony with ECK, in harmony with life.

The Secret Teachings, Mahanta Transcripts, Book 3, p. 225

This all fits in with the Law of Economy, because you get what you need. As a child you don't have many choices. As you grow older, you should have more. We look for spiritual freedom, and this also means we must have freedom of choice. The further we go along the path of ECK and the higher we go into the worlds of God, the more choice we expect to have....

The spiritual principle is that you get the most effect out of everything you do, and everything is turned to a spiritual effect. Through doing the spiritual exercises, the forces are no longer being scattered all over and wasted; they are now aligned in one direction, and that direction is home to God, to the Sugmad. So you see that the Law of Economy is important. What usually isn't noticed is that the Law of Economy is expressed in everything we do and in the people we meet every day.

The Secret Teachings, **Mahanta Transcripts, Book 3, p. 226**

We know that the world economy hasn't been operating on the Law of Economy. America is one of the great offenders. How long can you run without paying your debts? Some governments feel they can always start up the presses and print more money. There is a law against people doing this in their basement, but this is how many national governments operate—because they don't realize how the Law of Karma works.

The life of a country spans many decades, and karma doesn't necessarily come back tomorrow morning; it sometimes takes several years. In the meantime, everybody thinks they are getting a free ride. But they are forgetting the basic Law of Economy, which is the Law of Cause and Effect. You pay for everything you get, both spiritually and materially.

The different countries of the world act like many human beings. They simply don't understand the laws. The ECKist is among the chosen and enlightened who understands, at least in his head if not in practice, that sometime he must pay his debt—if not sooner, then later.

The Secret Teachings, **Mahanta Transcripts, Book 3, p. 228**

When something isn't carried out the way I'd like, the first thing I do is ask, Where's my responsibility in this? Is it possible I didn't communicate this clearly enough? Very often this is true. Working as we do at all the different levels, and with all the different languages we speak, communicating with each other can be quite difficult. As we go higher in ECK, our communication with Spirit becomes clearer. And hopefully, as we go further along the path, the communication among initiates should be cleaner and clearer.

An aspect of the Law of Economy is recognizing the weaknesses in any system on earth. This includes recognizing the weaknesses in our own character and makeup and working with them, as well as recognizing the same traits in other people and trying to work with them.

The Secret Teachings, **Mahanta Transcripts, Book 3,**
pp. 232–33

Take your share of drubbings, because within each lesson is hidden the seed of truth which is needed for you to take the step that follows. But you can't take the next step until you take the step that is right here. You must begin where you are now. When you can live your life fully, under the Law of Economy and the Law of Love, you will be qualified to take the next step.

The Golden Heart, **Mahanta Transcripts, Book 4, p. 144**

We can kid ourselves all we want, but the spiritual law is that we have to pay, in some way, for everything we get. This comes under the Law of Economy, which operates in the lower worlds up to the Mental Plane. Higher laws, such as the Law of Love, prevail in the spiritual worlds, but down here we are in the worlds of dichotomies—lack or plenty, highs and lows, riches and poverty.

Karma and reincarnation come under the Law of Economy. If you direct your spiritual energies in the most straightforward way, always keeping in mind where you are going, you will get through these rebirths faster than if you get sidetracked.

You pick a goal, such as God-Realization. Then you open yourself to the Holy Spirit, the ECK, and make your way directly through life to accomplish the goal. There will be help along the way. You take it as it comes, even though it may not seem to fit into your beliefs up to that time.

The Law of Economy starts down here in the physical.

The Golden Heart, **Mahanta Transcripts, Book 4,**
pp. 125–26

Facsimiles

Facsimiles, Law of. The sixth law of the physical universe; that all effects in life are brought about by the thoughts and pictures in the mind of the individual.

ECKANKAR Dictionary, **p. 51**

Facsimiles deal with those pictures you took in the mind. These pictures have been with you since you came into the world. They are filed away by Soul like cards in a little niche in the Soul's body. . . . Generally, facsimiles are either borrowed or they are one's own. One can have either or both through a compulsive basis or on an unknowing basis. They will influence him in one way or another. . . .

These facsimiles are merely little units of energy which gather about the body, mind and Soul. They keep the attention of the individual "I" on them, especially if they are bothersome pictures. This is what oriental religion keeps calling Karma.

The Flute of God, **p. 96**

The flows of energy which are recorded in facsimiles are dead flows. In order for them to have any power or life, a new flow of attention must be played over them by the individual. So you see that no matter what is wrong with the individual, he is the one who is keeping it that way. This comes in with cause and effect. When one is on a low level, he fails in his beingness. He is existing on death wishes, with qualities of unbeingness. The chief aspects of cause and effect are the positive and negative. When an individual is cause he is being positive; when he is effect he is being negative. The art of good picturization is the art of full beingness.

The Flute of God, pp. 96–97

Invisible Laws

The seven principles of consciousness . . . are as follows: 1. Appreciation, 2. Sincerity, 3. Unselfishness, 4. Idealism, 5. Devotion, 6. Personal effort, and 7. Attainment.

These are the invisible laws. . . . For example— 1. Appreciation is—appreciation of the teacher; 2. Sincerity is—to inspire the seeker to seek higher levels of consciousness; 3. Unselfishness—the willingness to sacrifice the individual self to the universe; 4. Idealism—the faculty of perceiving spiritual values through a perfect pattern; 5. Devotion—to fill the mind and Soul with love, aspiration and giving of the self to universal consciousness; 6. Personal effort— spiritual motivating force of intelligence which is within all men; 7. Attainment—the reward for spirit action.

Dialogues with the Master, **p. 217**

Karma

Karma, Law of. The Law of Cause and Effect, action and reaction, justice, retribution, and reward, which applies to the lower or psychic worlds: the Physical, Astral, Causal, Mental, and Etheric Planes; the Law of Universal Compensation which is under the Law of Vibration; inflow and outflow; a matter of vibrations; one of the twelve laws by which the universes are sustained.

ECKANKAR Dictionary, **p. 80**

The universality of the Law of Karma is one of the chief factors which binds life together, and not only human life but animal, plant, and mineral life as well. All those compose one big family, with a complicated and inseparable history and an inseparable karma.

The Shariyat-Ki-Sugmad, **Book One, p. 132**

By and large, the Lord of Karma—not the individual—is responsible for selecting the family through which Soul enters the physical plane. Like a guardian who administers a trust on behalf of an infant, he arranges for Soul to join a family which offers the best prospect for spiritual unfoldment. In making that selection, he is under no obligation to consider the feelings or imagined rights of the person so involved.

To him, placement is a simple matter: The Law of Karma, which governs such stationing, is the law. It must be obeyed.

Child in the Wilderness, **p. 20**

Destiny controls the conditions at birth. Much of what an individual does after that is an exercise of free will. Free will may overcome the conditions of destiny, but first one must awaken his creative talents, through which he can then reshape his spiritual and material life.

To sum up, fate governs the conditions at a person's birth; free will allows a choice as to how he will move within and beyond them.

Child in the Wilderness, **p. 21**

There simply is no such thing as righteous anger. The ECK doesn't recognize any distinctions between anger for a cause and anger for no cause. Through the Law of Karma, the ECK impartially doles out justice whenever there is any imbalance of the emotions.

The Golden Heart, **Mahanta Transcripts, Book 4, p. 175**

When someone wants to be a healer and then takes on another's illness, this karma from the other person was earned. It is often because the individual did not know the laws of Spirit, or perhaps was under the control of one of the five passions of the mind: greed, anger, lust, attachment, and vanity. This is what causes our karma.

Journey of Soul, **Mahanta Transcripts, Book 1, p. 104**

People who practice psychic healing may get away with it for years, because the Law of Karma is in no hurry. Spirit has plenty of time; It's in no hurry to collect the debt that a man has created. A psychic healer may be very good for ten, twenty, even forty years; but then his health all of a sudden may go bad. The karma has come home; it must be paid. He doesn't know what happened, only that he can heal others but not himself. Furthermore, he doesn't know why it happened. He has absolutely no understanding that he violated the laws of Spirit.

How to Find God, **Mahanta Transcripts, Book 2, p. 41**

The greater you become in your state of consciousness, the quicker your acts come back to you. In the Bible, St. Paul spoke of this Law of Karma when he said, "Whatsoever a man soweth, that shall he also reap."

How to Find God, **Mahanta Transcripts, Book 2, p. 18**

Until you come onto the spiritual path, you generally have a lifetime or two behind you that you're paying off, so you can't make the connection between what you did wrong in the past and the payment that is now coming due. As you move along the spiritual path, the higher you go, the quicker it comes back. If you do something that stands between another person and God-Realization, you very quickly find out that you have broken a spiritual law. It comes back sometimes within a week, a few minutes, or even seconds. It comes quickly enough so that you know: Ah! This pain is the result of a lack of understanding of that spiritual law.

How to Find God, **Mahanta Transcripts, Book 2, p. 56**

When one has not attained the high states of spiritual consciousness, this Law of Karma does not come back immediately. The higher you go in your awareness, the quicker the law comes back. That's good in one way and bad in another. I'd say overall it's good because as soon as you cheat someone, for instance, the law strikes and you get the karma over with sooner. The higher you go, the narrower becomes the path—some call it the razor's edge.

People who do not really have any regard for the spiritual law may just be learning life, taking it as they find it, cheating, robbing, and having a good time. The law does not demand its payment sometimes for two, ten, twenty, or thirty years, or maybe not until the next lifetime. When the payment doesn't come due as soon as the violation of the spiritual law is committed, the person thinks he's getting away scot-free. But there must be full payment in the true coin for every action.

How to Find God, **Mahanta Transcripts, Book 2,**
pp. 157–58

I can help you with some of the burdens, but I won't take them all from you. A debt to God that has been created must be repaid by the one who incurred the debt. This is the Law of Life: Whatsoever a man sows, that also shall he reap.

How to Find God, **Mahanta Transcripts, Book 2, p. 179**

One of the benefits of the path of ECK is that much of our karma can be worked off on the inner planes so that we don't have to go through it here. If we've created debts, they must be repaid to God. But on the path of ECK we have this advantage: They do not always have to be worked out here on the physical; they can be worked off on the inner planes in the dream state.

How to Find God, **Mahanta Transcripts, Book 2, p. 185**

We have been spoon-fed with ideas of a God who will heal us no matter what we do wrong. Some people think all they have to do is ask. They feel they can give advice to others that might destroy their lives, and by saying, God, please forgive me, it will all be forgotten. Unfortunately these people are ignorant of the spiritual law. St. Paul said, "Whatsoever a man soweth, that shall he also reap," and it means just that. You can kid yourself. A person can eat wrong until it affects his health and then reason that he can always find a doctor who will take care of him. Or he may ask God for a healing. And if it doesn't work he thinks, God didn't heal me; therefore, the God of this faith must not be right. In truth he has incurred a debt to Spirit; he himself must pay it back. No one can help him except himself.

How to Find God, **Mahanta Transcripts, Book 2, p. 214**

Nature

laws of nature. The laws of the negative power; the laws of the physical universe; the natural laws.

ECKANKAR Dictionary, **p. 87**

Now the law of the world as we know it is this: If a man's attention is focused upon an object which gives him pleasure, he will have pain if it is removed.

So you see, this law of nature compels us to place the attention of many on a permanent object so that there will not be an unbalancing of the emotions too greatly through pleasure or pain.

Dialogues with the Master, **p. 79**

While on Earth man is subject to the laws of the negative power, or what is often termed "The Laws of Nature."

Dialogues with the Master, **p. 167**

The Law of Nature tells us little or practically nothing about nature but certainly something about man. Assertions about the world are really assertions about ourselves. What man experiences in the ordinary course of life relatively is nothing but the Absolute experienced in a special way.

Dialogues with the Master, **p. 221**

Polarity

Polarity, Law of. The Law of Opposites. The third law of the physical universe; the state of opposition between any two related factors; yin and yang (negative and positive), feminine and masculine; the negative, or reactive, side and the positive, or active, side; the third part is the passive, or middle, path; each thing within this universe is supported, animated, maintained by, and is in opposition to its opposite.

ECKANKAR Dictionary, **pp. 114–15**

Polarity simply means the state of opposition between any two related factors: light and darkness, heat and cold, material and immaterial, harmony and discord, positive and negative, north and south, male and female, etc.

The Flute of God, **p. 88**

Anyone who lives on this side of the Law of Polarity is not free, but is one who is always reacting to circumstances, who is enslaved to reactive habits, who is always being exploited, and is desirous of materialistic factors. . . .

When one gains perfect knowledge of the Spirit, he does not have to give up the physical body and subtle bodies at once. He has his choice of going on living here

65

as long as he is in perfect harmony with Spirit as its agent and is not bothered with the law of the Opposites.

The Flute of God, pp. 88–89

This law states that every phenomenon, on whatever scale and in whatever world it may take place, from molecular to cosmic phenomena, is the result of combining the meeting of the two, plus the third, which is the passive middle. This is not the passive element that you find in negation, but a balancing of the two. It is the path which Buddha called the "Middle Path". . . .Scientific thought today realizes the existence of positive and negative forces. . . . But science has never raised the question of a third force. According to exact divine science, one force, or two forces, can never produce phenomenon. The presence of the third is always necessary to produce any phenomenon. This neutral force is not easily accessible to direct observation and understanding.

The idea of the unity of the three in Absolute ECK forms the basis of the three worlds and of the ancient teachings.

The Flute of God, p. 89

Within this material universe the Law of Polarity, or the Law of Opposites, operates. Nothing exists except in relation to its opposite. This is also true within the psychic worlds: Astral, Causal, and Mental. However, within the heavenly worlds this is not true; for here it is true that there are no opposites, although the sacred scriptures of the worlds say so.

These scriptures claim that the good go into some heavenly paradise while the evil will be punished forever in some fiery region. This is the Law of the Opposites, or Polarity. Those who are good attract the good, and those who are evil attract the evil. Therefore, in the heavenly states, it's found that polarity or chemistry within two objects no longer exists, and that Soul is free to do whatever It desires as long as it falls within a general pattern of the heavenly law. This law is: Love is all, and do as thou wilt.

The Shariyat-Ki-Sugmad, Book Two, p. 138

When Soul enters into the regions of immortality, or worlds of true Spirit above the psychic worlds, It finds no opposites. Light is light and there is no opposite to it and the sounds of ECK, only the polarity of the highest qualities. Therefore, the ECKist is a realist, for he knows how to use the Law of Polarity. When he has to use his consciousness in the psychic world, he is able to take advantage of the Law of Opposites. But when he is in the world of the true Kingdom of God, then he is able to use the Law of Polarity for his own benefit through this conscious state.

The Shariyat-Ki-Sugmad, Book Two, pp. 138–39

One of these laws is: "Nothing can exist except in relation to its opposite." This is an age-old principle of the positive and negative. The positive is the outgoing, the God force; and the negative is the inert, receptive force.

For example, laughter must have its opposite, tears; and neither can the universe have complete joy without sorrow. Therefore, this universe is not static, but is a constant dynamic state. There is nothing eternal on this plane but change itself. This is where God arrives in our lives, for behind the change lies the

67

eternal, the unchanging which the outer eye cannot see. As long as anything exists on the mental and physical plane, it is due to be in constant change.

Now, the second principle is, "That the positive is forever transforming into the negative and correspondingly, the negative is forever in the process of becoming the positive.". . .

Each power needs the other in this world. Without one the other could not exist. . . . The teachings need to be revitalized and reformed to show the world how to take advantage of the two forces, not to put a strain upon the individual aspirant to hold to one constantly, when it is almost an impossibility unless he is trained by the ECK Master. Therefore, do not despair if the cycle strikes in a low depression at one time, and then later turns to the higher, and vice-versa.

Dialogues with the Master, **p. 47**

Beyond the Soul Plane in those worlds of Spirit, we begin to work in the whole. There are no regions or planes that we know of; it is simply one world of Light. In the lower regions where we exist now, something can be known only by its counterpart—truth by untruth, light by darkness. At the Soul Plane as this ECK Stream, or Spirit of God, comes down from the God center, It splits into two parts: the positive and the negative. We have manifestations of this split, and though we take it for granted, it shows up all around us. If you want to iron, you first put the plug into the wall outlet, and this uses alternating currents—the positive and the negative. We see the height of the mountains and the depths of the valleys, because the only way anything can be known in these lower worlds is in comparison to its opposite. We're always thinking in parts.

The Greek philosophers came close to having the spiritual viewpoint. They tried to have an overview when they looked at life as it existed here, and they would address it from the whole. In the West, we fragment it—man and woman, happiness and sadness—and generally view life in its parts.

How to Find God, **Mahanta Transcripts, Book 2,**
pp. 182–83

Reversed Effort

Reversed Effort, Law of. The functioning of the imagination by negation which draws into the external that which one is trying to avoid.

ECKANKAR Dictionary, p. 125

For example the Law of Reversed Effort is simply that the harder a person struggles to achieve some goal, the more difficulty he will have to overcome; difficulty caused, at least in part, by the strain of his effort. "You try too hard; relax, take it easy, and try again," is an expression we hear so much in the Western world. We must make the mind one-pointed, as the Eastern adepts say, but nothing mental should be strained. We should never try to force results. We should stick to our task and finish out the race, but never knock ourselves out doing it.

ECKANKAR—The Key to Secret Worlds, p. 156

This is known in ECK as the Law of Reversed Effort! This law is a practical law of nature concerned only with man, for man is the only animal on earth that can make use of his imaginative powers! This law is concerned with the imagination. It goes like this: The more you try to put your imaginative powers upon something in concentrated effort, the less you can do it. The harder one struggles to achieve some goal, the more difficulty he will have to overcome; difficulty caused, at least in part, by the strain of his effort. "You tried too hard, relax, take it easy, and try again," are frequently heard expressions. It means to try not to force results!

Take, for example, when one is trying to ride a bicycle through rocks on a road, trying to avoid hitting the large ones, he is so conscious of hitting the rocks he'll probably do so. Or if a man tries to walk across a small plank from one building to another at the tenth floor, his mind would be on falling and not on the walking. You see this law is concerned with imagining and feeling! What you image must have feeling— therefore the negative imaging is more likely to be effective than the positive imaging because the negative has feeling with it!

Letters to Gail, **Volume I, p. 35**

Of course, any situation, when altered by force, will tend to persist. This is why so many people fail to resolve their problems, no matter who might be helping them. Force will make the problem and situation more solid regardless of whatever resolve there is to change them. Generally, the greater an untruth is in these circumstances, the more solid it will become if force is used.

The Key to ECKANKAR, **p. 37**

Unity

Unity, Law of. The seventh law of the physical universe; thinking in the whole instead of the parts.

ECKANKAR Dictionary, p. 154

The Seventh Law of the physical universe is: The Law of Unity, thinking in the whole instead of in parts. It is a simple way of knowing the solution to the problem the instant it presents itself. In a way this is called liberation from the bondage of the world, which men have always cried to their God to give them.

This law simply means that one must be wholly within the ECK in order to enjoy himself as the whole man and be able to select consciously what he wants in life and work at it.

The Flute of God, p. 97

Some of the ancient Greek philosophers used to think from the whole. They would consider the overview. Western man usually thinks in terms of the parts. Most people think only in fragments; and because they do, they can't step back and take a look at the whole situation, so a problem defeats them before they've taken even one step.

How to Find God, Mahanta Transcripts, Book 2, p. 336

Vibration

Vibrations, Law of. The fourth law of the universe which governs all the influences such as wavelengths, outflows, inflows, cause and effect, and the harmonics of the movement of sound.

ECKANKAR Dictionary, **p. 159**

The fourth law of this universe is the Law of Vibration, or Harmonics: This is the law that governs all the influences upon the Soul and body in this world, such as wavelengths; outflows from the planets, stars, and heavenly bodies; music; sound; color; and general harmonics. Under this principle falls karma, cause and effect and inflow and outflow.

The Flute of God, **p. 90**

Close observance shows the manifestation of the Law of Harmonics in vibrations of every kind including light, heat, chemistry and other vibratory sciences.

The Flute of God, **p. 91**

From the seven scales of music, each octave, do-re-mi-fa-sol-la-ti contains a good foundation for understanding the cosmic laws of vibrations. Each octave has an ascending octave, in which frequency of vibrations increase. ... As one goes along the scale, it is found to descend, after ti, and continue going around the scale again and again, until it makes a circle or something similar to a circle. This is true of the physical universe for nothing keeps a straight line.

The Flute of God, pp. 91–92

Nothing in the physical world stays in the same place, or remains what it was; everything moves, everything is going somewhere, is changing inevitably, either develops or goes down, weakens or degenerates.... Ascent or descent is the inevitable cosmic condition of any action.

The Flute of God, p. 92

   Pain and the past are nothing more than love's chrysalis, its shell, its seedbed, in which these necessary nothings
release such real wonders, such as the comforting thrill of
God's hand on one's shoulder.

Laws of Charity

The laws that bring Soul a greater capacity to love.

Chela, Laws and Rules for the

The laws and rules for the ECK chela are simple. These are to give harmony, purity, and perfection of Soul. This constitutes heaven while in the physical vehicle.

The Shariyat-Ki-Sugmad, **Book One, p. 100**

He must practice the disciplines of ECK. The first is to have cleanliness of mind, that no words which would pollute the air enter into his mind. He shall look upon all men as creatures of God and this only; for they, like himself, are temples who shall eventually become Co-workers with God.

He must, in mind, fast continuously from all Kal thoughts which could infect his mental state and consciousness. Through this he learns the powerful awareness of the presence of the Living ECK Master, who is with him constantly. He learns not to be deceived or dismayed by the conflicting world around him. He knows that all universes, regardless of whether or not they are under the rulership of the Kal Niranjan, are really worlds of perfection, harmony, and good.

He learns that patience is the greatest discipline of all the spiritual works of ECK. By patience he can endure life, hardships, karmic burdens, the slanders of men, and the pricks of pain and disease. He keeps his mind steadfastly upon the Light of God, never swerving, never letting up on his attention to the goal of God-Realization.

He comes to know humility and chastity in his life on earth and that all his responsibility belongs to God, not to anyone nor anything within this physical realm. His loved ones, family, and relatives are the images of God, mirrored in this worldly life and embodiment to serve the Sugmad, the Supreme Deity. . . .

He will come to discriminate between all things, that there is no good nor evil, no beauty nor ugliness, and there is no sin. That all these are concepts of the mind, the dual forces in the matter worlds. Once he recognizes and understands this, he will then be free of all the Kal traps.

He will be ready to enter into the Kingdom of God, the Ocean of Love and Mercy.

He will be the ECK, of Itself.

The Shariyat-Ki-Sugmad, **Book One, pp. 100–101**

The path of ECK doesn't eliminate the five passions of the mind; we learn how to control them. How? By focused attention, the power of Soul, which is ignited by the chanting of your word. By chanting your word, you instantly have the power to raise yourself in consciousness to the point where you are able to step back from any situation so that it doesn't overwhelm you. Then you can look at it objectively and unemotionally, and figure out what's happening. Ask yourself: Is it in my best interest? or Is someone using his creative imagination to trap me within the dimensions of his time and space?

How to Find God, **Mahanta Transcripts, Book 2, p. 287**

To live in this truth, to abide in the Word, is to bear the harvest of all things in the richest manner: that is, to live harmoniously in the spiritual senses.

The Key to ECKANKAR, **p. 40**

Creativity

Creativity, Law of. Every atom is striving continually to manifest more life; all are intelligent, and all are seeking to carry out the purpose for which they were created.

ECKANKAR Dictionary, p. 29

Life is a mystery until we come to the path of ECK. We begin to understand that we can be the creators of our own world and that, in truth, what we are today is a creation of that which we have made from the past. There is a way to change the future, and we can do it. But you don't do it by wishing.

When an individual looks for God-Realization, it has to be more than a passing fancy. It's not like a fashion that you only wear for a season; you don't just forget your high aspirations for God. It must be something that is within your heart in a gentle way. You know that no matter what happens on the path, it is always to lead you closer to the source of Soul's creation in the heart of God. Soul wants to return home.

How to Find God, **Mahanta Transcripts, Book 2, p. 31**

You develop a sense of humor, and as challenges come up, you begin to draw on your creativity. You find solutions that would never have occurred to you before. Life becomes more fun—you actually have a more adventuresome life. You get put into situations you would not have been in before, because you are

going one step beyond yourself. And as you get yourself in trouble, you also have help to get out of it,
because as you learn to work with your own resources,
you are developing self-mastery.

How to Find God, **Mahanta Transcripts, Book 2, p. 81**

Shakespeare says a poet's function is to reach to
heaven for ideas and bring them down to earth. It is
true that thought does not originate with man, but in
heaven. Where did Beethoven go to find his Fifth
Symphony? Did Jesus originate the Sermon on the
Mount? When great poetry and great music inspire
you, what is conceived, gestated, and born of that? You
can choose between noble and ignoble. You understand poetry and music. Love them, and let them flow
into your consciousness. So you see that we all are
linked to the sun, moon, and stars. We can lift our
consciousness to higher planes and see from above, as
if from the masthead of a ship, the past, present, and
future, all in a moment, through the eyes of Soul.

The Key to ECKANKAR, **p. 27**

Thought creates form, but it is feeling that gives
vitality to thought.

Thought without feeling may be constructive as in
some engineering work, but it can never be creative
in the work of an artist, or a musician. In all that
which originates within itself a new order of causation
needs to be recognized, a creation, the inner twined
reality of thought and feeling. It is this inseparable
union of thought and feeling that distinguishes creative thought from analytical thought and places it in
a different category. If one is to utilize a new starting
point for carrying on the work of creation, it must be

84

done by assimilating the feeling of the Divine ECK into the pattern of one's thought by entering into the stream of the ECK.

The images in the mind from the stream of the spirit have to be generic. By its very nature the principle of life must be prolific, tending to multiplicity, and the original thought image must be fundamental to the whole race, not limited to particular individuals. Consequently the image in the stream of the ECK must be an absolute type containing the true essentials for the perfect development of the race. This is the perfect substance of the thing in thought.

Therefore, it is that our unfolding as centers of creative activity, as exponents of new laws, and through them of new conditions, depends on our realization that Divine Power is the archetype of consciousness perfection, at once as thought and feeling.

The Flute of God, pp. 125–26

Danda, the Righteous Law

danda. *DAHN-dah* Self-discipline; sometimes called the righteous law. It treats the divine rights of people as well as kings; works both ways, neither can trespass upon the other's rights.

ECKANKAR Dictionary, **p. 31**

Those of you who wish to make the effort can also attain this self-mastery in life. You do not come to the point where you begin to direct or control Spirit, because Spirit will not be controlled or directed. People who try to do this are using the psychic powers, black magic. Instead, you let Spirit flow through you without any blocks or obstacles whatsoever. Eventually you become Its pure vehicle, as an ECK Master; and whatever It wants, you carry it out. When you get a direction on the inner planes, you immediately begin figuring ways to carry it out. Sometimes it may take a while. You pick priorities and begin working on them.

How to Find God, **Mahanta Transcripts, Book 2, p. 81**

When you come to the state of self-mastery, it does not mean that you now have license to live life doing whatever you please. It simply means that now you know and understand the laws of Spirit as they apply to you. You know the things you can do and the things you cannot do. And while you make your way through

87

life with these guidelines, you also are being a vehicle for Spirit.

How to Find God, **Mahanta Transcripts, Book 2, p. 177**

A Christian who lives the Law of Righteousness is far superior to a chela who engages in useless arguments with other chelas about whether there is dogma in Eckankar. Even though we are ultimately on a path that is centered upon the inner reality of truth, we do need the outer expression of truth while in a human body.

The Living Word, **p. 77**

The righteous law is called danda. It treats the divine rights of the people as well as that of kings. When it works both ways, it means that neither can trespass upon the other's rights. To have to write law upon the books and use this as a guide to keep society within the moral standards of life is to bring about disorder in a society. As the human race enters upon its decline in civilized standards, there is, and was, a transfer of the center of government from within man to enacted statutes; in other words, from moral standards deeply embedded in the inner consciousness of people to laws written in books. When the time came that the fundamental danda, the Law of Righteousness, was no longer in the hearts of people but in books, then the decline of civilization set in for society.

It is only the ECK Masters who have witnessed such changes and have tried to lift the human race above the decline of every civilization in the history of mankind. The task is hard but since the Golden Age, long since passed, every ECK Master who has spent time upon this earth has gone through the Silver

Age, the Copper Age, and others to witness the degenerative changes. Slowly has come the Iron Age, which marks the lowest ebb in individual and social degeneration. It is during this period that modern laws, governments, and social regulations began to appear. Men, supposedly wise in nature, hailed these changes as progress. But it's not true that man has progressed in nature, but has decreased due to the workings of the Kal forces. He usually does not recognize such a negative force and, if he does at all, he scorns it as being nothing in his life.

The Shariyat-Ki-Sugmad, Book Two, pp. 77–78

Dharma

dharma. *DAHR-muh* The Law of Life; the righteousness of life; doing what is right; the code of conduct that sustains the right ethics in life.

ECKANKAR Dictionary, **p. 34**

One takes for granted before he starts on the path of ECK that he is to become well grounded in the fundamentals of righteousness. He must practice the dharma, the Law of Life itself, in all aspects of his life. This means doing what one ought to do while an ECK chela. Without doing this he cannot make a start in life.

The Shariyat-Ki-Sugmad, **Book One, p. 139**

Karma, of course, is bound up with reincarnation. It is separated into two parts: cause and righteousness, which are the basic factors that create karma. It is the disobedience of the Law of Dharma, which is rightness or righteousness, the law of life or what ought to be done, that brings about karma for the individual or groups.

The Shariyat-Ki-Sugmad, **Book Two, p. 78**

It should always be borne in mind that ignoble thoughts and actions inevitably result in unhappy consequences.

The Key to ECKANKAR, **p. 16**

91

The negative power, or Satan, is merely an instructor who is in charge of God's earthly schoolroom, the place where Soul gains purification so that It may one day reenter the heavenly states of consciousness and become a Co-worker with God.

You and I—Soul—were created in the heart of God and put in the lower worlds because we simply would not serve others. We were self-serving, enjoying our life on the Soul Plane and other worlds, and we would not give anything in any way. And so we came into the lower worlds.

Many of you write and ask, "What is my mission in life?" Very specifically, it is to become a Co-worker with God. How this breaks down for your particular talents is actually between God and you.

How to Find God, **Mahanta Transcripts, Book 2, p. 7**

Another point is to live the karmaless life. To act without creating further karma is to do everything in the name of God or in the name of that Inner Master within you. This is a simple way to go through life.

How to Find God, **Mahanta Transcripts, Book 2, p. 9**

We are interested in learning how to live life fully, not how to contemplate and withdraw, or retreat, from life. By living fully, we get the experience we need to one day become a Co-worker with God. You need every conceivable experience. It's better to go out and do something that you would later find was wrong, than to do nothing. At least you learned something—even if it's only that you would never do it again—and you're smarter than you were before.

How to Find God, **Mahanta Transcripts, Book 2, p. 80**

There is no easy way to explain the teachings of ECK and the truth contained therein. That understanding has to be an individual undertaking. The most we can do for our family is to ask for their goodwill in letting us study the path of our choice. Give them the same freedom and just enjoy each other as people and as loved ones. Sometimes we're able to work it out, sometimes not.

I really don't like the teachings of ECK to come between members of a family, and I certainly don't recommend anyone take the ECK discourses on the sly, such as through an anonymous post office box. That's being dishonest. In the spiritual life you find you have to be honest. We don't look to ethics as our goal, we look to God-Realization: but as we gain in spiritual unfoldment, our ethics do become greater— more so than on any other path.

How to Find God, **Mahanta Transcripts, Book 2, p. 108**

All I'm concerned about is that the outer life stays in harmony and balance and that you don't go out there and do strange things all of a sudden—give up your job, take all your savings out of the bank, and go off to an ashram. That is not the spiritual life. The spiritual life is carrying out the duties that we have accepted, such as family and children, and figuring out ways to support them. This is where the challenge of life is today.

How to Find God, **Mahanta Transcripts, Book 2, p. 144**

One of the spiritual principles that I have learned is that there is always a way, no matter what. If we have a health, financial, or some other kind of situation—there is always a way out.

How to Find God, **Mahanta Transcripts, Book 2, p. 175**

Four Zoas

The four Zoas (laws) of Eckankar for the Mahdis, the initiate of the Fifth Circle, are: (1) The Mahdis shall not use alcohol, tobacco, drugs, gamble, or be gluttonous in any way. No Mahdis shall be existent on the animal level. He is a leader, and he must fix his attention above the psychology of the brute. (2) The Mahdis shall not speak with tongue of vanity or deceit or unhappiness, criticize the actions of others, blame others for wrongdoings, quarrel, fight or inflict injury. He shall at all times be respectful and courteous to his fellowman and show great compassion and happiness. (3) The Mahdis shall have humility, love, and freedom from all bonds of creeds. He shall be free from the laws of karma which snare him with boastfulness and vanity. He shall have love for all people and all creatures of the Sugmad. (4) The Mahdis must preach the message of ECK at all times, and prove to the world that he is an example of purity and happiness. He must show that the disciple in the human body must have a Master in the human body. This is a fixed law of the Sugmad. At the time of his passing, every Living ECK Master turns over his work to the next Living ECK Master who is in the body, and he carries on until his time to translate from the human body into the other worlds. Those who translate shall continue with the ECK chelas they have initiated on earth, when those chelas have passed across the borders of death into the upper worlds.

Their ECK Master meets them, and they begin their further studies under him in the heavenly worlds.

These are the four laws for the Mahdis, the initiate of the Fifth Circle. They shall be abided by and shall have the respect given to the Mahanta, for each law within itself has great authority and power. The works of Eckankar depend mainly upon the Mahdis.

The Shariyat-Ki-Sugmad, Book Two, pp. 51–52

Love

Love, Law of. The principle which gives thought the dynamic power to correlate with its object, and, therefore, to master every adverse human experience; feeling that imparts vitality to thought; feeling is desire, and desire is love.

ECKANKAR Dictionary, **p. 90**

Before you leave this life, take the trouble to learn the secret doctrine of ECK. It is the Law of Love which alone can carry you to God.

The Living Word, **p. 229**

The law of love will bring to you the necessary materials for your spiritual growth and maturity.

Therefore, if you require love, try to realize that the only way to get love is by giving it, that the more you give the more you get, and the only way in which you can give it is to fill yourself with it until you become a magnet of love.

Simplified, the mechanics of love is this: Thought is a channel of emotions and is carried by the Law of Vibration, the same as light or electricity. It is given vitality by the emotions through the Law of Love; it takes form and expression by the Law of Growth; it is a product of Soul and hence it is divine, spiritual and creative in nature.

Dialogues with the Master, **p. 140**

Since we know that we cannot love everybody equally, then we can love warmly only a certain number, but according to the law, we must give impersonal love to all.

Dialogues with the Master, p. 18

There are many routes we can take to heaven. God has established so many different paths and means for us that there is a way for everyone, including the atheist. This sounds almost like a humorous paradox, but it's true. An atheist can be closer to God than a Bible-carrying, born-again Christian, simply because the atheist may have a better understanding of the Law of Love.

The Golden Heart, Mahanta Transcripts, Book 4, p. 85

Every man must first seek to give love if he expects to receive it. He must give it under every circumstance—even though he is abused, mistreated, and given unnecessary hardships in this world.

The Shariyat-Ki-Sugmad, Book One, p. 133

You must choose to love only those who will be faithful in returning a love to you, and who will not use your love for a selfish purpose. This is the use of discrimination in your love for your fellow man.

Dialogues with the Master, p. 18

The subjective can change conditions because it is a part of the universal mind and a part must be the same as the creative power of the ECK Power. This (as everything else) is governed by God Law, and this Law is the Law of Love, which is God-Power in creation, which automatically correlates with its objects and brings it into manifestation.

Dialogues with the Master, **p. 122**

We blame our problems on the Kal Niranjan, which, of course, is our own base nature. To put it another way, the Kal is our indulgence run free. It is perhaps more honest to look at Kal Niranjan, the king of the negative world, as something of our own creation which has no life or energy except what we give him.

In other words, I'm pointing the finger right back at the person—which is usually ourself—who sends out the blast of energy to other people. We are responsible for all the ripples created in others by our anger, as well as the ripples they in turn pass along to the next group. The higher you go as an initiate in ECK, the greater your responsibility becomes. The Law of Love becomes very exacting.

The Golden Heart, **Mahanta Transcripts, Book 4, p. 176**

Of course, there is an even greater law, and this is the Law of Love. This is the Law of Spirit, the Light and Sound of God. You can bring It into your own life, and when you do, there will be no one who can take It from you or tell you this or that way is right for you. You are going to know for yourself from direct experience with the Light and Sound of God.

How to Find God, **Mahanta Transcripts, Book 2, p. 179**

You find that spiritual ecstasy does not touch all. But those whom it does touch, feel love drenching all consciousness, overwhelming all being. Love is God, and love is an act of God. Memories, doubts, and fears are far away when perceived through love, dimmed by love that is in itself so absolute, so separate from logic, that nothing else matters. Death is only an incident. Tortures can be endured until one dies, but it does not matter. In the end, agony dies of its own nothingness, like irrecoverable years. Love lives forever! Pain and the past are nothing more than love's chrysalis, its shell, its seedbed, in which these necessary nothings release such real wonders, such as the comforting thrill of God's hand on one's shoulder.

The Key to ECKANKAR, p. 26

Knowledge can bring many things, for knowledge comes from mind expansion, but the consciousness of the heart brings love, and love brings all things.

The Key to ECKANKAR, p. 29

Noninterference

Even the Living ECK Master does not enter into somebody's personal affairs without definite permission. The spiritual law forbids it.

The Wind of Change, **p. 162**

The lesson was that a spiritual being cannot violate the personal space of others, even if he is desperate to make a living.

Child in the Wilderness, **p. 253**

Anyone who uses any means of change or influence on another's mind, including prayer, is violating a law of spiritual consciousness.

ECKANKAR—The Key to Secret Worlds, **p. 219**

When we see another person with problems and troubles, we can have compassion; but we understand that somewhere down the path these problems have come to him by his own efforts. We let him have the freedom to have his troubles. If he asks for help or compassion in one sense or another, we can give it, but we certainly do not interfere with another person's problem and take it on ourselves by saying, I'm going to pray for his healing. We learn the laws of Spirit.

How to Find God, **Mahanta Transcripts, Book 2, pp. 40–41**

The Living ECK Master will never interfere in your life at any time, because your state of consciousness is like your home — it's a violation of the spiritual law for anyone to walk in without your permission. The troubles we have are of our own making, through our own ignorance of these spiritual laws. These laws are at work whether or not we are conscious of how they work.

How to Find God, **Mahanta Transcripts, Book 2, p. 73**

One is required to pay the price for breaking the spiritual laws even though it is done in ignorance. This is the highest law. "Do unto others as you would first have them do unto you" really means if I don't want people meddling in my life without permission, then I ought to extend that same privilege to others.

How to Find God, **Mahanta Transcripts, Book 2, p. 165**

Silence

kamit. *KAH-mit* The Law of Silence, which means being silent about the secret teachings, personal affairs with ECK, and the personal word given in the initiations.

ECKANKAR Dictionary, p. 79

A spiritual law, such as the Law of Silence, may be disarmingly simple on the surface, but its scope only becomes apparent when the individual tries to practice it. This particular law means to keep silent about whatever passes between the spiritual student and the Mahanta, who is the Inner Master: unless, of course, instructed otherwise by the Master. But people tend to overlook such laws, especially if the tests are given in their own backyards.

The Living Word, p. 36

The holy ECK, or the Word, must be practiced in silence. Only those who have received the Word in initiation can be given the blessings of the Sugmad through the Mahanta. The practice of the personal secret word of each initiate shall be done vocally when alone or silently while in public. He shall practice not only the kamit, the Law of Silence, with his secret word but shall practice the silence in his own affairs with ECK, and whatever is given him in the secret teachings.

The Shariyat-Ki-Sugmad, **Book One,** p. 163

We must work for our own spiritual unfoldment. There will be no cheerleaders applauding on the sidelines. Hardly anyone will be aware of our experiences in the Sound and Light of ECK as we obey the Law of Silence. The inner initiations may come years before the pink slip that invites us to complete the cycle of the initiation on the physical plane.

The Living Word, p. 234

The Law of Silence is good. It's best not to wear our troubles on our shirtsleeve where other people can look at and discuss them. The ECK Masters tell us: Forget gossip; it's something you don't need. It may seem as if they're saying they don't want us to gossip because somehow it's not upstanding, it's not spiritual—it's just that all those mental concepts don't mean anything to us.

Journey of Soul, **Mahanta Transcripts, Book 1, pp. 79–80**

When a person wants to know about your experiences in ECK, you don't have to get into a big explanation. You can observe the Law of Silence and simply tell them: "It's not important what experiences I have, but what you have." Just give them an ECK book and say, "Try the spiritual exercises. . . . If you find they work for you, great—the path has something to offer you. If not, then maybe it's not for you. But try it for yourself."

How to Find God, **Mahanta Transcripts,** *Book 2,* **pp. 98–99**

104

Glossary

Words set in SMALL CAPS are defined elsewhere in this glossary.

ARAHATA. An experienced and qualified teacher for ECKANKAR classes.

CHELA. A spiritual student.

ECK. The Life Force, the Holy Spirit, or Audible Life Current which sustains all life.

ECKANKAR. Religion of the Light and Sound of God. Also known as the Ancient Science of SOUL TRAVEL. A truly spiritual religion for the individual in modern times, known as the secret path to God via dreams and SOUL TRAVEL. The teachings provide a framework for anyone to explore their own spiritual experiences. Established by Paul Twitchell, the modern-day founder, in 1965.

ECK MASTERS. Spiritual Masters who can assist and protect people in their spiritual studies and travels. The ECK Masters are from a long line of God-Realized SOULS who know the responsibility that goes with spiritual freedom.

HU. The most ancient, secret name for God. The singing of the word HU, pronounced like the word *hue,* is considered a love song to God. It is sung in the ECK Worship Service.

INITIATION. Earned by the ECK member through spiritual unfoldment and service to God. The initiation is a private ceremony in which the individual is linked to the Sound and Light of God.

LIVING ECK MASTER. The title of the spiritual leader of ECKANKAR. His duty is to lead SOULS back to God. The Living ECK Master can assist spiritual students physically as the Outer Master, in

105

the dream state as the Dream Master, and in the spiritual worlds as the Inner Master. Sri Harold Klemp became the MAHANTA, the Living ECK Master in 1981.

MAHANTA. A title to describe the highest state of God Consciousness on earth, often embodied in the LIVING ECK MASTER. He is the Living Word.

PLANES. The levels of heaven, such as the Astral, Causal, Mental, Etheric, and Soul Planes.

SATSANG. A class in which students of ECK study a monthly lesson from ECKANKAR.

THE SHARIYAT-KI-SUGMAD. The sacred scriptures of ECKANKAR. The scriptures are comprised of twelve volumes in the spiritual worlds. The first two were transcribed from the inner PLANES by Paul Twitchell, modern-day founder of ECKANKAR.

SOUL. The True Self. The inner, most sacred part of each person. Soul exists before birth and lives on after the death of the physical body. As a spark of God, Soul can see, know, and perceive all things. It is the creative center of Its own world.

SOUL TRAVEL. The expansion of consciousness. The ability of SOUL to transcend the physical body and travel into the spiritual worlds of God. Soul Travel is taught only by the LIVING ECK MASTER. It helps people unfold spiritually and can provide proof of the existence of God and life after death.

SOUND AND LIGHT OF ECK. The Holy Spirit. The two aspects through which God appears in the lower worlds. People can experience them by looking and listening within themselves and through SOUL TRAVEL.

SPIRITUAL EXERCISES OF ECK. The daily practice of certain techniques to get us in touch with the Light and Sound of God.

SUGMAD. A sacred name for God. Sugmad is neither masculine nor feminine; It is the source of all life.

WAH Z. The spiritual name of Sri Harold Klemp. It means the Secret Doctrine. It is his name in the spiritual worlds.

Bibliography

ECKANKAR Dictionary. 2d ed., 2d printing. Minneapolis: ECKANKAR, 1973, 1989.

Klemp, Harold. *The Book of ECK Parables,* Volume 2. Minneapolis: ECKANKAR, 1988.

———. *Child in the Wilderness.* Minneapolis: ECKANKAR, 1989.

———. *The Golden Heart,* Mahanta Transcripts, Book 4. 2d printing. Minneapolis: ECKANKAR, 1990.

———. *How to Find God,* Mahanta Transcripts, Book 2. Minneapolis: ECKANKAR, 1988.

———. *Journey of Soul,* Mahanta Transcripts, Book 1. 2d printing. Minneapolis: ECKANKAR, 1988.

———. *The Living Word.* 3d printing. Minneapolis: ECKANKAR, 1989.

———. *The Secret Teachings,* Mahanta Transcripts, Book 3. Minneapolis: ECKANKAR, 1989.

———. *The Wind of Change.* 4th printing. Minneapolis:ECKANKAR, 1980.

Twitchell, Paul. *Dialogues with the Master.* 9th printing. Minneapolis: ECKANKAR, 1970.

———. *ECKANKAR—The Key to Secret Worlds.* 2d ed., 2d printing. Minneapolis: ECKANKAR, 1969, 1987.

———. *The Flute of God.* 10th printing. Minneapolis: ECKANKAR, 1969.

————. *The Key to ECKANKAR.* 2d ed., 3d printing. Minneapolis: ECKANKAR, 1968, 1985.

————. *Letters to Gail,* Volume I. 6th printing. Minneapolis: ECKANKAR, 1973.

————. *The Shariyat-Ki-Sugmad,* Book One. 2d ed., 3d printing. Minneapolis: ECKANKAR, 1970, 1987.

————. *The Shariyat-Ki-Sugmad,* Book Two. 2d ed. Minneapolis: ECKANKAR, 1971, 1988.

————. *The Spiritual Notebook.* 2nd ed., 3d printing. Minneapolis: ECKANKAR, 1971, 1990.

For Further Reading and Study*

Journey of Soul
Mahanta Transcripts, Book 1
Harold Klemp

This collection of talks by Eckankar's spiritual leader shows how to apply the unique Spiritual Exercises of ECK—dream exercises, visualizations, and Soul Travel methods—to unlock your natural abilities as Soul. Learn how to hear the little-known Sounds of God and follow Its Light for practical daily guidance and upliftment.

The Spiritual Exercises of ECK
Harold Klemp

This book is a staircase with 131 steps. It's a special staircase, because you don't have to climb all the steps to get to the top. Each step is a spiritual exercise, a way to help you explore your inner worlds. And what awaits you at the top? The doorway to spiritual freedom, self-mastery, wisdom, and love.

ECKANKAR—Key to Secret Worlds
Paul Twitchell

This introduction to Soul Travel features simple, half-hour spiritual exercises to help you become more aware of yourself as Soul—divine, immortal, and free. You'll learn step-by-step how to unravel the secrets of life from a Soul point of view: your unique destiny or purpose in this life; how to make personal contact with the God Force, Spirit; and the hidden causes at work in your everyday life—all using the ancient art of Soul Travel.

35 Golden Keys to Who You Are & Why You're Here
Linda C. Anderson

Discover thirty-five golden keys to mastering your spiritual destiny through the ancient teachings of Eckankar, Religion of the Light and Sound of God. The dramatic, true stories in this book equal anything found in the spiritual literature of today. Learn ways to immediately bring more love, peace, and purpose to your life.

*Available at your local bookstore. If unavailable, call (612) 544-0066. Or write: ECKANKAR Books, P.O. Box 27300, Minneapolis, MN 55427 U.S.A.

There May Be an
Eckankar Study Group near You

Eckankar offers a variety of local and international activities for the spiritual seeker. With hundreds of study groups worldwide, Eckankar is near you! Many areas have Eckankar centers where you can browse through the books in a quiet, unpressured environment, talk with others who share an interest in this ancient teaching, and attend beginning discussion classes on how to gain the attributes of Soul: wisdom, power, love, and freedom.

Around the world, Eckankar study groups offer special one-day or weekend seminars on the basic teachings of Eckankar. Check your phone book under **ECKANKAR**, or call **(612) 544-0066** for membership information and the location of the Eckankar center or study group nearest you. Or write **ECKANKAR, Att: Information, P.O. Box 27300, Minneapolis, MN 55427 U.S.A.**

☐ Please send me information on the nearest Eckankar center or study group in my area.

☐ Please send me more information about membership in Eckankar, which includes a twelve-month spiritual study.

Please type or print clearly.   940

Name _____
      first (given)   last (family)

Street_____ Apt. # _____

City _____ State/Prov. _____

ZIP/Postal Code _____ Country _____